BUDDHIST
Prayer and Worship

Adiccabandhu and Anita Ganeri

W
FRANKLIN WATTS
LONDON•SYDNEY

First published in 2006 by
Franklin Watts
338 Euston Road
London NW1 3BH

Franklin Watts Australia
Level 17/207 Kent Street
Sydney NSW 2000

Editor: Rachel Cooke
Design: Joelle Wheelwright
Picture research: Diana Morris

Acknowledgements:
The prayers on pages 7, 9, 12, 13, 19 and 29 come from *Puja: The FWBO Book of Buddhist Devotional Texts*, © Windhorse Publications 1999.
Photographs: Ask Images/Ark Religion: 12. Tibor Bognar/Ark Religion: front cover r, 27. British Museum, London/Topfoto: 24. Clear Vision Trust: 18. Nick Dawson/World Religions Photo Library: 22. Bennett Dean/Eye Ubiquitous: 10-11. Sarah Errington/Hutchison: 16. Fortean Picture Library/Topfoto: 23. Michael Freeman/Corbis: 26. Fiona Good/Ark Religion: 19. Patricio Goycoolea/Hutchison: 21. Houghton/Topfoto: 15. Nigel Howard/ Hutchison: 6, 17. Jenny Matthews/Franklin Watts: 20. Christine Osborne/World Religions Photo Library: 4, 9. Tim Page/Eye Ubiquitous: 28. Helene Rogers/Ark Religion: 29. Phil Schermeister/ Corbis: 5. Paul Seheult/Eye Ubiquitous: 14. Sean Sprague/Image Works/ Topfoto: 25. Claire Stout/World Religions Photo Library: front cover bl, 8. Malcolm Watson/Ark Religion: 13. Julian Worker/ World Religions Photo Library: 7.
Every attempt has been made to clear copyright. Should there be any inadvertent omission please apply to the publisher for rectification.

A CIP catalogue record for this book is available from the British Library.

Dewey Decimal Classification Number: 294.3

ISBN 978 0 7496 5935 6

Printed in China

Franklin Watts is a division of Hachette Children's Books

Contents

The prayers in this book were chosen by Adiccabandhu, a member of the Western Buddhist Order. This is a new Buddhist movement started by an English Buddhist, Sangharakshita, in 1967. It draws its teachings from many different Buddhist traditions. A primary school teacher and author of many children's books about Buddhism, Adiccabandhu was ordained nine years ago. He is currently Chairman of the Blackburn Buddhist Centre in England.
The prayers were chosen from different Buddhist traditions to show the great variety of Buddhist worship.

About Buddhism

Buddhists are followers of Buddhism, one of the world's major religions. It began in northern India about 2,500 years ago with the teachings of Siddhartha Gautama, a royal prince who became the Buddha. Buddhists use his teachings as a guide for their lives and as a way to understand how life truly is.

The Buddha teaching some of his first followers.

Buddhist beliefs

Buddhism is unusual because, unlike other religions, it is not based on a belief in a personal God who created the world and watches over it. The Buddha did not claim to be a god and did not expect to be worshipped as one. Rather, he was an extraordinary person who became enlightened. He realised the truth about how things really are. He then spent his life teaching people the way to Enlightenment. The Buddha taught that people make themselves unhappy by always wanting more than they already have. He showed people a path to follow to free themselves from suffering and find happiness.

We are what we think.
All that we are arises
with our thoughts,
With our thoughts we
make the world.
Speak or act with a
pure mind,
And happiness will
follow you
As your shadow,
unshakeable.

About this prayer
This passage comes from the Dhammapada, a popular collection of the Buddha's sayings. It is part of the Tipitaka (or Pali Canon), the sacred texts of the Theravada Buddhists. These verses remind Buddhists that they must work to change themselves through karma. This means doing things to help themselves and others. Karma can be good or bad actions. Good karma leads a person towards Enlightenment. Bad karma takes them further away.

Buddhists around the world

From India, Buddhism spread to many parts of Asia. In each country, it has adapted to local customs and traditions. More recently, it has become more popular in Europe, North America and Australia. Today, there are about 350 million Buddhists. There are many different groups of Buddhists but all Buddhists share the same basic beliefs.

A Buddhist temple in Hawaii. Buddhism is practised in many places around the world.

Buddhist Prayer and Worship

There are many different forms of Buddhist worship. Buddhists can worship both at home or in a temple or monastery, on their own or in groups. Worship means paying respect and saying thank you to the Buddha, chanting or reciting verses from the sacred texts and meditating (see pages 20-23). Buddhist worship is often called puja, an Indian word for showing respect.

A Buddhist worshipping at a shrine at home.

Worship at home

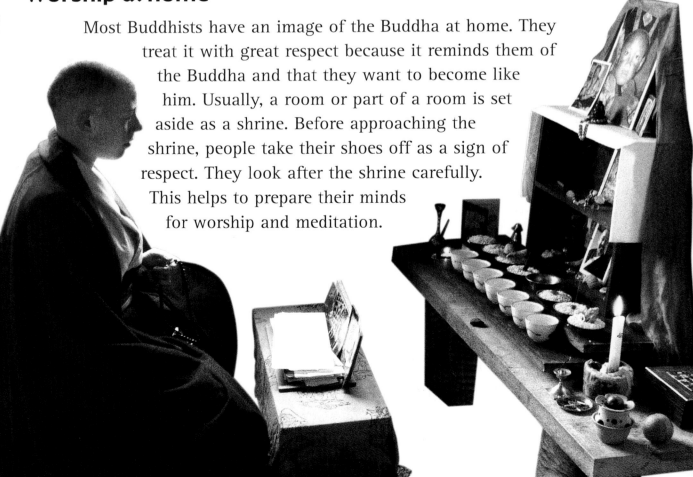

Most Buddhists have an image of the Buddha at home. They treat it with great respect because it reminds them of the Buddha and that they want to become like him. Usually, a room or part of a room is set aside as a shrine. Before approaching the shrine, people take their shoes off as a sign of respect. They look after the shrine carefully. This helps to prepare their minds for worship and meditation.

Worship in the temple

Some Buddhists meet and worship in a temple or monastery. There, they spend the time quietly, meditating, or taking part in puja.

In the temple's shrine room, Buddhists may kneel and bow three times in front of the image of the Buddha. They also put their hands together and imagine that their fingers are forming a cluster of lotus petals around a jewel standing for Enlightenment. All these actions show respect to the Buddha. By showing respect, Buddhists believe that they will learn more from the Buddha.

Then the puja ceremony begins: people make offerings to the Buddha and repeat their commitment to him and his teachings (see page 4).

Buddhists worshipping together in a temple.

*We reverence the Buddha
and try to follow him.
The Buddha was born
As we are born.
What the Buddha overcame,
We too can overcome.
What the Buddha attained,
We too can attain.*

About this prayer

This verse is part of the puja ceremony. In the temple, it may be recited in Pali, an ancient Indian language. At home, Buddhists may recite it in their own languages as part of their private worship. The verse shows respect for the Buddha and reminds Buddhists that, with the right effort, everyone has the ability to be like the Buddha and gain Enlightenment.

Sacred Words

There are many different sacred texts in Buddhism, linked to the various traditions and groups. Some texts contain the Buddha's teachings. Others are writings by later Buddhist monks and enlightened teachers. Buddhists believe that the sacred texts hold the words of truth, whether they have come from the Buddha or from another teacher. Reciting passages from the sacred texts is an important part of Buddhist worship.

A verse in Pali from the Tipitaka.

The Tipitaka

The Tipitaka are the sacred texts of the Theravada Buddhists. From the time of the Buddha, monks and nuns met twice a month to recite the Buddha's teachings. This helped them to remember them. The word 'Tipitaka' means 'Three Baskets' because the texts were later written down on palm leaves, stored in three 'baskets' or collections. Theravada

Buddhists believe that the Tipitaka contain the actual sayings of the Buddha and give his guidance on how to reach Enlightenment. Many passages from the Tipitaka are used in Buddhist worship. When Buddhists recite the texts, they take great care to say them accurately because they are so important. The Tipitaka are written in Pali.

Sacred sutras

Mahayana Buddhists have their own sacred texts called 'sutras'. They are believed to be the very words of the Buddha and are treated with great respect. It is thought that even hearing a sutra being recited is a great blessing. It is like being in the presence of Enlightenment. Most of the sutras were written down in the ancient Indian language of Sanskrit. Later, they were translated into other languages, such as Tibetan, Chinese and Japanese.

Buddhist monks study the sacred texts in Myanmar (Burma).

Here then,
Form is no other
than emptiness,
Emptiness no other
than form.
Form is only emptiness,
Emptiness only form.

Feeling, thought,
and choice,
Consciousness itself,
Are the same as this.

About this prayer

This passage comes from the Heart Sutra, a famous Mahayana Buddhist text. This sutra is thought to set out the teachings of the Buddha in a very short form. It is sometimes recited in Sanskrit or in English as part of puja. When Buddhists recite these words, they believe that they are opening their hearts to the truth. The sacred texts are a way for Buddhists to know the truth. But the real meaning of the passage is that the truth is beyond words.

The Three Jewels

As part of their daily worship, Buddhists repeat their commitment to the Three Jewels of Buddhism. These are the Buddha; the Dharma, the Buddha's teaching; and the Sangha, the community of Buddhist monks, nuns and laypeople. They are called jewels because they are so precious to Buddhists.

The Buddha

The first jewel is the Buddha. For Buddhists, the Buddha jewel means that they have an ideal to follow in their lives. An ideal is something that is perfect. When Buddhists worship the Buddha, they focus their minds on his qualities of great kindness and wisdom. These are the most important values they try to have in their lives.

The Dharma

The second jewel is the Dharma, or the teachings of the Buddha. The Dharma jewel is the guide for how Buddhists should live their lives. It shows them how to achieve the values of great kindness and great wisdom. The greatest goal in a Buddhist's life is to make progress towards these values.

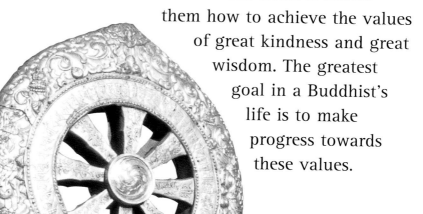

The Sangha

The third jewel is the Sangha, or the community of Buddhists. It is precious because it shows Buddhists that others can gain Enlightenment too. Members of the Sangha help each other to stay on the right path. For Theravada Buddhists, the Sangha means the Buddhist monks. They help ordinary Buddhists by teaching the Dharma. For Mahayana Buddhists, the Sangha means anyone who is trying to gain Enlightenment.

Buddhists represent the Dharma with an eight-spoked wheel. This one is on a monastery in Tibet.

I go to the Buddha for my refuge
I go to the Dharma for my refuge
I go to the Sangha for my refuge.

For the second time, I go to the Buddha for my refuge
For the second time, I go to the Dharma for my refuge
For the second time, I go to the Sangha for my refuge.

For the third time, I go to the Buddha for my refuge
For the third time, I go to the Dharma for my refuge
For the third time, I go to the Sangha for my refuge.

About this prayer

These verses are called the 'Refuge to the Three Jewels'. A refuge is somewhere safe. Buddhists recite them when they meet to meditate, at family ceremonies (see page 29), and at daily puja. They say the verses to show they are placing their trust in the Three Jewels as the source of true happiness. By reciting the verses three times, Buddhists feel that they are going for refuge with their bodies, their speech and their minds.

Making Offerings

To show their respect for the Buddha, Buddhists take offerings of flowers, candles and incense to the temple. They place them on the shrine in front of the Buddha's image. Each of these offerings has a special meaning, reminding worshippers of the Buddha and his teachings. Buddhists also make offerings when they perform puja in private at home.

A Buddhist offers flowers at a shrine.

Reverencing the Buddha, we offer flowers. Flowers that today are fresh and sweetly blooming, Flowers that tomorrow are faded and fallen. Our bodies, too, like flowers will pass away.

About this prayer

Offering flowers is an ancient Indian way of welcoming honoured guests. Long ago, when the Buddha visited someone's home, his host put a garland of flowers around his neck. This custom continues today. Flowers stand for the beauty of the Buddha's teachings. Flowers also remind Buddhists of a very important teaching - that everything, including ourselves, changes and that nothing lasts for ever. Like everything else, flowers eventually wilt and die. This teaches Buddhists that it is best to use their time well.

Verses of offerings

Making offerings is important in Buddhist worship because being generous is a very highly valued quality. If Buddhists visit other Buddhists, they always take a gift for them. When Buddhists give a gift, they believe that they are showing their joy at having their friends or families. When they make offerings to the Buddha, they show their joy at having the Buddha's teachings. As Buddhists make their offerings, they chant the verses you can read below.

Buddhists often offer candles at a shrine.

Reverencing the Buddha, we offer candles.
To him who is the light, we offer light.
From his greater lamp, a lesser lamp we light within us,
The lamp of Bodhi shining within our hearts.

About this prayer

When the Buddha went to stay with friends, they would give him a lamp or candle to light up his room. For Buddhists, candles are a symbol of the Buddha's Enlightenment. One way of explaining Enlightenment is that it is like a light going on in the darkness. The light stands for the wisdom that takes away the darkness of ignorance. When they offer candles, Buddhists remember that the Buddha's teaching lights up their lives and shows them the way to live.

*Reverencing the Buddha, we offer incense.
Incense whose fragrance fills the air.
The fragrance of the perfect life, sweeter than incense,
Spreads in all directions throughout the world.*

About this prayer

Incense was another gift given to the Buddha. Incense was used to freshen a guest's room and to keep mosquitoes away. Buddhists believe that, like the sweet smell of incense, the Dharma spreads everywhere and that even their smallest actions have an effect on others. Buddhists often light a stick of their favourite incense to make the room smell pleasant before they meditate. Buddhist children like to wave incense sticks to remind them that every act of kindness helps to make the world a better place.

Incense and other offerings on a Buddhist shrine.

Other offerings

Apart from flowers, candles and incense, Buddhists can offer anything beautiful on the shrine. This might be a particularly pretty pebble, a favourite poem, or even gifts of fruit or chocolate bars. It is a way for Buddhists to show their thanks to the Buddha for putting the goal of Enlightenment in their lives. They believe that a small act of gratitude like this will help them to become more generous.

A variety of offerings on a Buddhist shrine, including fruit.

I offer mountains made from precious stones, And forest groves to be enjoyed in solitude, Vines blazing with flowers, And trees whose branches hang low with delicious fruit.

About this prayer

This verse comes from a Buddhist text written hundreds of years ago called the 'Path of the Bodhisattva' by a monk called Santideva. It is often used by Mahayana Buddhists. It may be said in any language. It is really saying, 'I have nothing of my own to give but, if I could, I would give all the beautiful things in the world. If I owned the world, I would give it all.' When Buddhists recite this verse, they feel pleasure in every beautiful thing that they see. They feel that these things are made more beautiful by the Buddha's teachings. Being happy to give helps Buddhists overcome the feeling of wanting to have things for themselves.

The Five Precepts

Whenever they recite the 'Refuge to the Three Jewels' (see page 11), Buddhists also chant the Five Precepts, or Promises, below. These are five guidelines for living which all Buddhists try to follow to show their commitment to the Three Jewels. Buddhist parents teach their children how to follow these five rules.

Many Buddhists chant the Refuge and Precepts together before they meditate.

I undertake to abstain from taking life.
I undertake to abstain from taking the not given.
I undertake to abstain from bodily misconduct.
I undertake to abstain from false speech.
I undertake to abstain from taking drink and drugs that cloud the mind.

*Abstain means to stop yourself from doing something.

About this prayer

The Precepts are about how to treat ourselves and others with respect. For Buddhists, the first Precept is the most important. The other four Precepts are guides to how Buddhists can achieve the first one. The first Precept is about being kind at all times. Buddhists believe that it is never right to be angry because it makes the world a sadder place for everyone. The Buddha said that anger, ignorance and wanting things were the main causes of suffering. By following the Precepts, Buddhists hope to change these into kindness, wisdom and generosity.

Five positives

Each of the Five Precepts also has a positive side. These show the way that Buddhists would like to live. The Five Positives are:

'I will try to be kind to all beings.

I will try to give generously.

I will try to be content with what I have.

I will try to speak truthfully and kindly.

I will try to keep my mind clear at all times.'

The Five Positives help to develop compassion, generosity, contentment, kind and truthful speech, and mindfulness or awareness, all of which are important qualities for Buddhists. Some Buddhists chant the Five Positives whenever they chant the Five Precepts.

Most Buddhists are vegetarian because they feel it is unkind to kill animals to eat.

Rules for monks and nuns

In their daily lives, Buddhist monks and nuns must follow a set of rules about how to live and behave. The rules include the Ten Precepts which are the Five Precepts followed by laypeople, together with five extra rules. Monks and nuns have to follow stricter guidelines than ordinary people because they vow to live lives of purity, and to give up their possessions and careers.

17

Sevenfold Puja

In the temple or monastery, Buddhists like to meet together for special puja ceremonies. One of the best-known is called the Sevenfold Puja. This puja is performed by Mahayana Buddhists all over the world. It is also performed by Buddhists in Tibet. It is seen as a way of showing their wish to gain Enlightenment in order to help other beings.

Seven stages

This puja is called 'sevenfold' because it has seven stages or sections. Each section is devoted to different qualities that Buddhists want to develop. These qualities are: respect, commitment, shame for any wrong-doing, delight in the good of others, openness to the truth, and a desire to live more for others. Each section has its own verses which remind Buddhists of these qualities.

Western Buddhists taking part in the Sevenfold Puja. Buddhists also perform puja at home.

A Buddhist prostrates himself in front of the Buddha.

May the merit gained
In my acting thus
Go to the alleviation of the
suffering of all beings.
My personality through
out my existences,
My possessions,
And my merit in all three ways,
I give up without regard
to myself
For the benefit of all beings.

Just as the earth and
other elements
Are serviceable in many ways
To the infinite number of beings
Inhabiting limitless space;
So may I become
That which maintains all beings
Situated throughout space,
So long as all I have not
attained to peace.

During the puja, worshippers make offerings of flowers, candles and incense (see pages 12-13). Some Buddhists in Tibet also prostrate themselves before the shrine. This means lying down flat on the floor, and folding their hands in prayer above their heads. By doing this, they are worshipping with their whole bodies.

About this prayer

These are the last verses of the Sevenfold Puja. By reciting these verses, Buddhists express their wish to use any merit, or good, gained from their own actions to save other beings from suffering. Mahayana Buddhists believe that they are not only trying to gain Enlightenment for themselves but for everyone. Thinking of others is a very important quality for all Buddhists.

19

Meditation

Meditation is an important part of Buddhist worship. The Buddha himself gained Enlightenment while he was meditating. Buddhists like to meditate every morning before they start their day. Meditation means clearing and calming the mind so that it becomes peaceful and rested. By meditating, Buddhists become more aware of themselves and other people. They remember that everything they do and say has an effect on other people.

! *A group of children learn to meditate.*

What is the way to practise?
The person who wants to
practise goes to a forest place,
Or the foot of a tree, or a hut,
or to any quiet place, and sits
cross-legged.
He sits upright and alert. He
trains himself like this;
'I am breathing in and I am
aware of my whole body.
I am breathing out and I am
aware of my whole body.'
This is how he practises.
'I am breathing in and making
my whole body calm and
at peace.
I am breathing out and
making my whole body calm
and at peace.'
This is how he practises.

About this passage

This is the Buddha's teaching on meditation. It comes from a talk called 'The Sutra on the Full Awareness of Breathing'. It is not a prayer but it is sometimes read as part of worship to help Buddhists hear the Buddha's teaching and think about it. If Buddhists listen with an open heart, the teaching will go deeper.

A Japanese Zendo (place of meditation).

Learning to meditate

To meditate, Buddhists can sit on a stool or cushions, or cross-legged on the floor. They may meditate on their own or in groups. Buddhists sit upright so that they can stay alert but close their eyes. Then they gently relax their bodies. They pay special attention to how they are breathing. As they do this, they gradually become calm and quiet inside.

Meditation helps Buddhists to slow everything down and to see more clearly. This seeing is wisdom. Meditation is not easy because our thoughts get in the way. It takes plenty of practice to learn to let these thoughts go. But anyone can meditate. They do not need to be Buddhists.

Being mindful

The Buddha also taught his followers how to be mindful, or aware. In their daily lives, Buddhists try to be aware of themselves and how they are feeling inside. This helps them to be calmer in difficult situations. It keeps their minds fixed on their aim of living by the Buddha's teachings. If they are calm, they are less likely to become angry or worried, and they will be able to be more aware of others and act more kindly towards them.

Breathing calmly

One way of being mindful is to be aware of how you are breathing as you go about your daily tasks. You will begin to breathe calmly and evenly. Another way is to walk calmly and slowly wherever you go. Buddhists sometimes imagine a lotus flower springing up with every step they take. In one story, when the Buddha took his first steps as a baby, lotus flowers sprung up in his footprints.

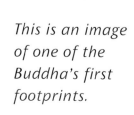

This is an image of one of the Buddha's first footprints.

22

Loving kindness

For Buddhists, metta, which means 'loving kindness' is the greatest quality of all. As they meditate, Buddhists practise sending out loving thoughts to others. In their minds, they gently repeat phrases like, 'May all beings be happy', or 'May all beings be well'. Some Buddhists like to repeat these phrases over and over during the day. By doing this, they hope to become kinder in their daily lives.

A group of Western Buddhists meditate on stools or cushions, with blankets wrapped around their waists.

*May all beings
be happy.
May all beings be well.
Weak or strong,
Large or small,
Seen or unseen,
Here or elsewhere,
Present, or to come,
in heights or depths.
May all beings
be happy.
May all beings be well.*

About this prayer

This prayer is called the Metta Sutta. It comes from the Tipitaka (see page 8) and is the advice given by the Buddha about how to practise metta. Buddhists believe that we can be kind whoever we are, wherever we are and whomever we are with. When they practise metta, they send kind thoughts out into the world. There are five stages to these kind thoughts – kind thoughts for ourselves, for our good friends, for people we feel comfortable with, for people we find difficult, and finally, for all beings. Buddhists believe that it is very important to be kind to everyone, even to people we do not like!

Chanting Mantras

Many Buddhists worship by chanting sacred words, called 'mantras'. A mantra is a special phrase or sentence. Buddhists say a mantra to themselves, or chant it out loud, over and over again. It is a form of meditation.

In Tibet, the mantra 'Om mani padme hum' is often carved or painted on stones.

Om mani padme hum

About this prayer

This is a very famous mantra chanted by Tibetan Buddhists. It is written in the ancient Indian language of Sanskrit. The mantra can have several different meanings. One meaning is 'Om, the jewel in the lotus'. Most mantras begin with 'Om'. Buddhists believe that chanting this word helps to open up their minds. The jewel (mani) can mean Enlightenment and the lotus (padme) can mean everyday life or even at this very moment. So the whole mantra means that Enlightenment is possible right now.

Bodhisattvas

This mantra is chanted to Avalokiteshvara, the Lord of Compassion. He is one of many bodhisattvas – beings who have gained Enlightenment but, out of kindness and compassion, choose to help other people to find happiness. Some Mahayana Buddhists pray to bodhisattvas for guidance. They chant mantras to call on the bodhisattvas to help them live better, happier lives.

Counting mantras

Some Buddhists like to chant hundreds of mantras during the day. To help them concentrate and keep count, they use strings of beads. These strings of beads are called 'malas' which means necklaces. If Buddhists do not want to use mala beads, they might chant to the rhythm of their breathing or of their steps as they walk.

Flags and prayer wheels

In Tibet, Buddhists write mantras and other prayers on brightly coloured prayer flags. Buddhists believe that, when the wind blows the flags, it spreads the messages of kindness far and wide throughout the world. Some mantras are written out and placed inside huge prayer wheels. These wheels are called 'mani wheels' after one of the words of the mantra 'Om mani padme hum'. Spinning the wheels is said to release the mantras into the world. Some Buddhists like to carry small, handheld prayer wheels which they spin as they go about their daily lives.

Buddhists spin huge prayer wheels at a temple in Mongolia.

In Daily Life

Many Buddhists like to recite verses to themselves during the day. This helps them to remember the Buddha's teachings and to keep up their efforts to follow these teachings. Some of these verses are very short and are called gathas. A gatha is a verse that lifts up the heart.

Not to do evil,
But to do what is right.
To keep the mind pure.
This is the teaching of
the Buddha.

About this prayer

This is a famous gatha from the Dhammapada (see page 5). It sums up the key steps on the Buddhist path to Enlightenment. These are not doing evil, doing what is right and using meditation to purify the mind and gain wisdom.

A Buddhist nun reads from the Dhammapada.

Choosing a gatha

Any verse can be used as a gatha. Some Buddhists have a favourite which they like to recite throughout the day. Like the gatha opposite, this often comes from the Dhammapada. Some Buddhists also write their own gathas or copy them out of the holy books.

A gatha can be linked to a simple act that is repeated often during the day, for example opening a door or walking down a corridor. So every time a Buddhist does this, he or she may say a verse like, 'Again, I open the door of opportunity at this moment', or, 'Every step takes me closer to my goal'.

For Buddhists, prayer can be part of everyday acts such as sweeping the floor.

By the power and truth of this act may all beings have happiness and the causes of happiness.
May all beings be free from sorrow And the causes of sorrow.
May all beings never be separated From the sacred happiness which is sorrowless.
May all beings live in a state of calmness
Free from greed and anger.
And may all beings believe in the Equality of all that lives.

About this prayer
This prayer is part of a Tibetan prayer. It is used by many Buddhists who say it in Tibetan, English or in their own languages. Buddhists say this verse quietly to themselves as they wash up, sweep the floor or after meditation. They want their actions to help others and believe that this will help to make the world a better place.

Special Occasions

Buddhists do not have fixed times of the day for prayer or meditation, nor do they have set holy days in the week. But there are many special times for worship through the year.

Buddhists light oil lamps at Wesak.

Full Moon Nights

Many Buddhist festivals happen on nights when there is a full moon. This is when the most important events in the Buddha's life are said to have happened. Long ago, the Buddha's followers met on full moon nights to meditate and recite the Buddha's teachings. In some Buddhist countries, people still go to the temple or monastery to do this.

Wesak

The most important festival for all Buddhists is Wesak. It is celebrated on the night of the full moon in April or May. Some Buddhists spend the whole day quietly. They meditate, read about the Buddha and spend some time chanting. In the evening, they meet in the temple or monastery to perform a special puja to call the Buddha to mind. They may also share a meal.

May all blessings be yours;
May all gods protect you.
By the power of all the Buddhas
May all happiness be yours.

May all blessings be yours;
May all gods protect you.
By the power of all Dhammas
May all happiness be yours.

May all blessings be yours;
May all gods protect you.
By the power of all the Sangha
May all happiness by yours.

About this prayer

These verses of blessing come from
Theravada Buddhism. They are usually
chanted in Pali by a monk at ceremonies
to mark special times for a Buddhist
family. These may be a baby's naming
ceremony (above), or a wedding. On
these occasions, some Buddhists visit the
temple or monastery with their families.
Others invite a monk to their house to
lead the ceremony. The verses are also
used as a parting blessing when people
are about to go and live somewhere.
They can even be used at the end of
books like this one as a blessing from
the authors to the readers. They are a
way of saying a Buddhist goodbye!

Glossary

Bodhisattvas Heroic beings in Mahayana Buddhism who have gained Enlightenment and become Buddhas. Out of compassion, they choose to help other people overcome suffering.

Chant To half-sing, half-speak the words of a prayer. Chanting is very calming and peaceful to do and to listen to.

Dharma The Sanskrit word for the Buddha's teaching. The word dharma means 'eternal law' or 'teaching'. It is written as dhamma in the Pali language.

Enlightened A person who has understood the truth about the world and seen things as they really are. This is like waking up from a deep sleep.

Enlightenment The state of being Enlightened.

Five Precepts Five guidelines for living which all Buddhists try to follow. They are also called the Five Promises. Buddhist monks and nuns follow five extra rules.

Gathas Short verses from Buddhist sacred texts which many Buddhists like to recite as they go about their everyday activities. The verses help to remind them of the Buddha's teaching.

Incense Sticks of sweet-smelling spices which are lit as part of worship.

Karma The Sanskrit word karma means 'action'. It refers to people's good or bad actions which affect their future happiness. It is written as kamma in the Pali language.

Laypeople In Buddhism, members of the faith who are not monks or nuns.

Mahayana One of the main forms of Buddhism. Mahayana means 'the great way'.

Mantras A short prayer or verse which is chanted silently or out loud over and over again. Mantras are chanted as part of meditation.

Meditating A practice performed by Buddhists in which they make their minds calm and clear so that they become more aware of themselves and others.

Metta The quality of loving kindness. For Buddhists, this is the most important quality of all. When they practise metta meditation, they aim to send kind thoughts out into the world.

Pali An ancient Indian language in which the sacred texts of the Theravada Buddhists were first written down.

Puja An Indian word meaning giving honour or respect which is often used to describe Buddhist worship. This involves honouring the Buddha as an extraordinary human being.

Sangha The community of Buddhists which began with the Buddha's first followers. For some Buddhists, the Sangha particularly means monks and nuns. For others, it means all Buddhists everywhere.

Sanskrit An ancient Indian language in which many Mahayana sacred texts were first written down.

Sutras The Sanskrit word for short texts which are sacred to Mahayana Buddhists. The word sutra means 'thread'. It is also written as sutta in the Pali language.

Theravada One of the main branches of Buddhism. It means 'way of the elders'.

Three Jewels The Buddha, the Sangha and the Dharma. These three are called jewels because they are so precious to Buddhists.

Further information

Books to read
Puja: the FWBO book of Buddhist devotional texts
Windhorse Publications 1999

Sacred Texts: the Tipitaka and other Buddhist texts
Anita Ganeri, Evans Brothers 2003

Keystones: Buddhist Vihara
Anita Ganeri, A&C Black 1998

Religion in Focus: Buddhism
Geoff Teece, Franklin Watts 2003

Websites
www.buddhanet.net
A general site covering all aspects of Buddhism.

www.londonbuddhistvihara.co.uk
The website London Buddhist Vihara (a Theravada Buddhist place of worship).

www.fwbo.org
The website of the Friends of the Western Buddhist Order.

www.worldprayers.org
A collection of prayers from many different faiths and traditions.

Index